QUICK FIX SCIENCE

LIGHT

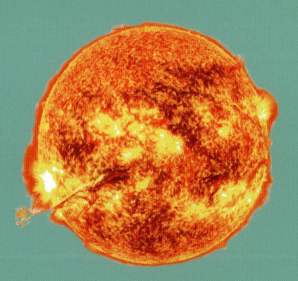

PAUL MASON

WAYLAND

First published in Great Britain in 2021
by Wayland
Copyright © Hodder and Stoughton, 2021
All rights reserved

Design: www.squareandcircus.co.uk
Editor: Nicola Edwards

HB ISBN: 978 1 5263 1585 4
PB ISBN: 978 1 5263 1586 1

Printed and bound in China

Wayland, an imprint of
Hachette Children's Group
Part of Hodder and Stoughton
Carmelite House
50 Victoria Embankment
London EC4Y 0DZ
An Hachette UK Company
www.hachette.co.uk
www.hachettechildrens.co.uk

Cover and interior Snappy artwork by John Haslam

Picture acknowledgements:
The publisher would like to thank the following for permission to reproduce their pictures:

Alamy: I4images rm 21b; Andrew Linscott 19tl; S Lyons Photography 18c.
© MBARI: 27bl.
Shutterstock: Kurit Afshen 25c; Altrendo Images 17t; Amenicl81 12b, 26t;
Aphelleon front cover tl, 5t, 3l; Beholding333 25br; 29b; Oleg Belov 29b;
Charlotte Bleijenberg 25bcl; Samuel Borges Photography 27t; Cerez 8t;
Marjan Cermelj 19c; Alex Cherepanov 21c; Crepesoles 7bl; Kate Cuzko 23tl;
EB Adventure Photography 9br; Emmily 4t; Evannovostro 28l; Ewa Studio 29tr;
Natalia Lukiyanova Frenta front cover tr; Fer Gregory 8bc; grey_and 23c;
I.C.E Photostock 25bcr; Sugrit Jiranarak 17b; John99 9tr; Kim7 6c;
Denis Kuvaev 22; May_Lana 4b; Leksi.photo 14b; Lucapd 23b; Maquiladora 10-11t;
Amy Newton-McConnel 2-3c, 20t; Nattika 23tr; Oleganko front cover c;
Oneinchpunch 28r; Vita Pakhai 5b; Pixfiction front cover trc;
Public House Design 10-11b; robert_s, elements furnished by NASA 1;
Fouad A Saad 20b; Maria Savenko 9bc; Savvapanf Photo 3tr, 9tl, 30;
Shablon 6b; Fabrika SImf 19br; Olha Solodenko 24cl, 24cr;
Somchai Som 8bl; Retesh Ssinha 25bl; Suzi44 9bcl;
TheFarAwayKingdom front cover b; Vadven 9bl; Nicholas Voisin44 19bc;
Winessyork 8br; Yanishevska 29tl; Vadim Zakharishchev 2lt.
Wikimedia Commons: Bostjan Burger/PD 26b; D J Johnston/CCA-SA 3.0 27br.

Every attempt has been made to clear copyright. Should there be any inadvertent omission
please apply to the publisher for rectification.

Meet Snappy.

Snappy is a young Nile crocodile.

Most crocodiles are only interested in eating and sleeping, but Snappy is different.

Snappy is interested in **science**, too.

CONTENTS

What is light?   4

A light experiment   6

Light sources   8

Day and night   10

Seasons   12

Light lines   14

Shadows   16

Reflections   18

Mirror images   20

Colours   22

Animal eyes   24

Light and life   26

Work it out   28

Glossary   30

Answers   31

Finding out more   32

Index   32

WHAT IS LIGHT?

I LOVE lying in sunlight – it's so warm. Bright light is also useful when I'm looking for my lunch: it helps me to see better. I sometimes wonder, though: what actually IS light?

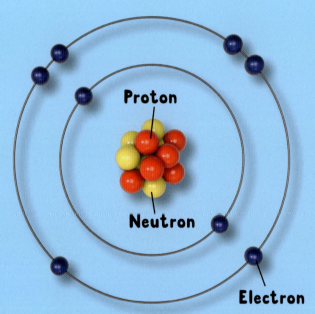

An atom

0.00001 mm

Light = energy

Light is a kind of energy. It is released by **atoms**, the tiny building blocks that all things are made of. We see this **energy** as light and sometimes feel it as heat.

If grains of sand were as big as the Singapore Flyer, atoms would be as big as grains of sand.

Light from the Sun

The Sun is a giant, super-hot ball of atoms. It gives off lots of light and heat – so much that looking at the Sun is dangerous.

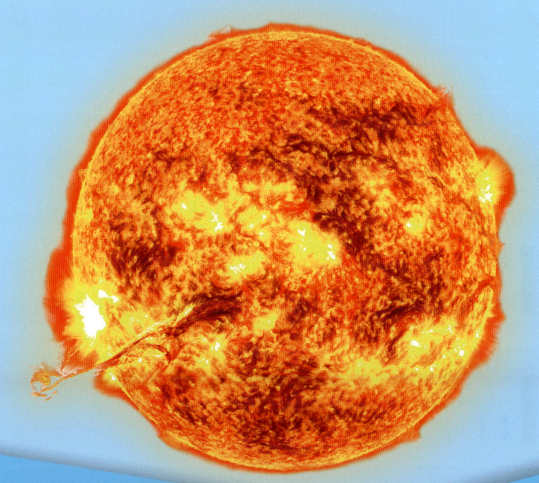

When you heat up atoms, they release light. For example:

Except crocodiles can't hold matches ... or candles.

A LIGHT EXPERIMENT

We can see things that give out light, or things that light bounces off. When there is no light, we can also see – or actually, NOT see – that …

Dark-tube experiment

1.

Put one end of the tube flat against the page, then put your eye right up against the other end.

How much can you read?

You need:

- this page
- black paper about 30–40 cm wide and 20–25cm long, made into a tube
- a torch
- a fat knitting needle.

2.

Use the knitting needle to carefully make a hole in the side of the tube, near the bottom. Shine the torch into it.

What changes?

3.

Turn the tube around so that the hole's at the top, and shine the light through it again.

What looks different?

After each step, see if you agree with the answers on page 31.

LIGHT SOURCES

Sometimes when the Sun's gone down and I should be asleep*, there's still light on my riverbank. I've often wondered where this comes from.

*crocodiles keep an eye open for danger even when we're asleep ...

The Sun is not the only thing that produces light. There are thousands of others. Some are made by humans. Others come from nature.

Do you know which of these things makes light? (Watch out! Some of them just bounce light back.)

Lightbulb

Firefly

Cat's eyes

Light and heat

Many **light sources** also give out heat. Some give out more heat than others:

10% of energy becomes light.
90% of energy becomes heat.

An old-fashioned lightbulb

Uses 25% as much energy
Produces almost no heat.

A modern lightbulb

Bicycle light and reflector

Angler fish

Phone screen

Solar tower

You can find out if you were right on page 31.

DAY AND NIGHT

Most light comes from the Sun. But at night there's no light from the Sun. Why is that? Does the Sun get turned off like a lightbulb?

Plink!

The Sun doesn't get turned off at night. In fact, the Sun will be providing us with light for at least another 5 billion years.

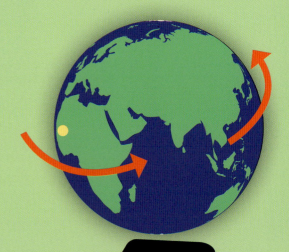

0700 hrs
MORNING

You're in Africa, where I live.

EARTH

SUN: Lots of very hot atoms

Why it gets dark at night

The reason the Sun appears and disappears each day is that the Earth is spinning. It does one full spin every 24 hours.

When your bit of Earth is facing toward the Sun, its light shines on you and it is daytime.

When your bit faces away from the Sun, it's dark and nighttime.

1200 hrs
MIDDAY

2000 hrs
SUNSET

Light and heat

SEASONS

Here in Africa, it's always warm during the day. Sometimes, we have VERY hot days that seem to go on for ages, though. I don't really know why this is …

In most parts of the world, days are longer and hotter in summer. This is because the Earth **tilts** towards and away from the Sun at different times of year.

DECEMBER

It is northern winter and southern summer.

The north gets less sunlight, so days are shorter and cooler.

North Pole tilts away from the Sun.

Sunlight

Poles same distance from the Sun

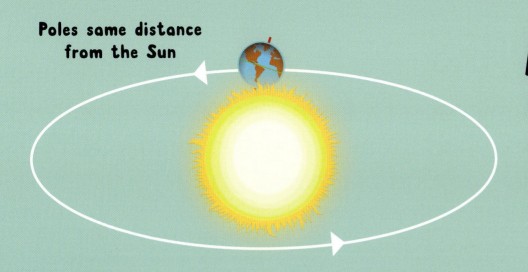

It is northern spring and southern autumn.

The north and south get the same amount of sunlight.

North Pole tilts towards the Sun.

Sunlight

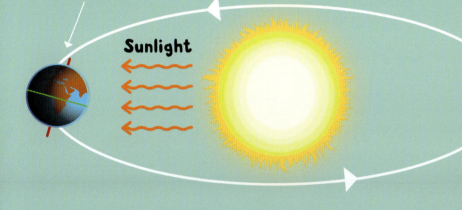

It is northern summer and southern winter.

Now, the south tilts away and gets less sunlight. Days here are shorter and cooler.

It is northern autumn and southern spring.

The north and south once again get the same amount of sunlight.

Poles same distance from the Sun

LIGHT LINES

In my country, Egypt, explorers once searched for amazing treasures in dark underground places.

Imagine if YOU were looking for hidden treasure in a deep, dark **tomb**. Which of the light sources on the right would be best?

Sunshine is very bright and the Sun never goes out ...

BUT... light travels in straight lines. It cannot turn corners, so it is no use on an underground treasure hunt.

You can take a box of matches anywhere ...

Candle lanterns last longer than matches ...

BUT... they are not very bright, and only last a few seconds. Plus, what if you set light to something in the tomb?

BUT... their light goes out to all sides. They are no good for seeing into hidden holes or finding secret latches.

A torch would last a long time and let you see into dark corners and holes. This is the number 1 explorer's choice.

The light from a torch travels straight to wherever you point it.

SHADOWS

I love lying in the sunshine to warm up. When I get TOO hot, though, I cool down in a shady place, or go for a swim and cover myself in cold, wet mud.

Light sometimes hits something it cannot pass through. An area of darkness, called a shadow, appears. Snappy cools down in the **shade** because less sunlight equals less of the Sun's heat, too.

Shadow-puppet shapes

Making shadow puppets is a great way to understand how light travels in straight lines, but is stopped by some objects.

Shadows change size depending on how close they are to the light source. You can test this by moving your hands closer and then further away from the torch. What happens to your shadow puppets?

You need a dark room and a bright torch.

Black and grey

In a dark place, one strong light makes a very dark shadow.

Most shadows are grey, not black. This is because a bit of light from other sources creeps into the shadow.

Light travels in straight lines, so shadows have the same shape as the objects that cast them.

REFLECTIONS

Sometimes, sleeping with one eye open is really annoying*. Like when a boat goes by ... the boat's lights bounce off the water and make an extra-bright disturbance.

*Crocodiles do this to watch out for danger.

Reflections happen when light hits something it cannot pass through. Not all reflections are the same. Try this experiment to see why:

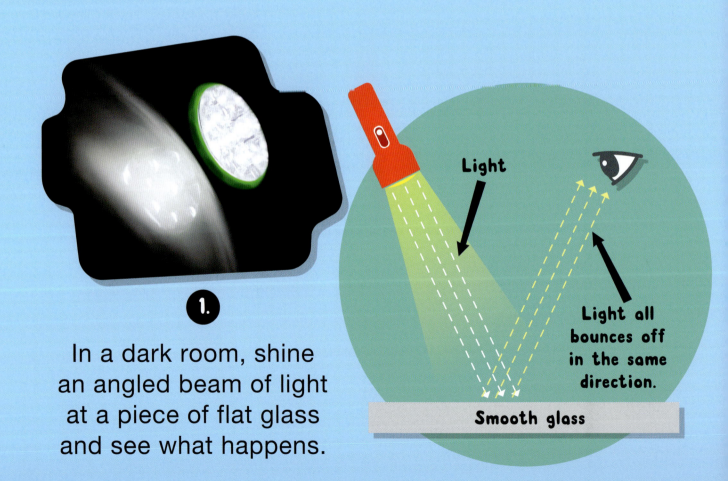

1.

Light

Light all bounces off in the same direction.

Smooth glass

In a dark room, shine an angled beam of light at a piece of flat glass and see what happens.

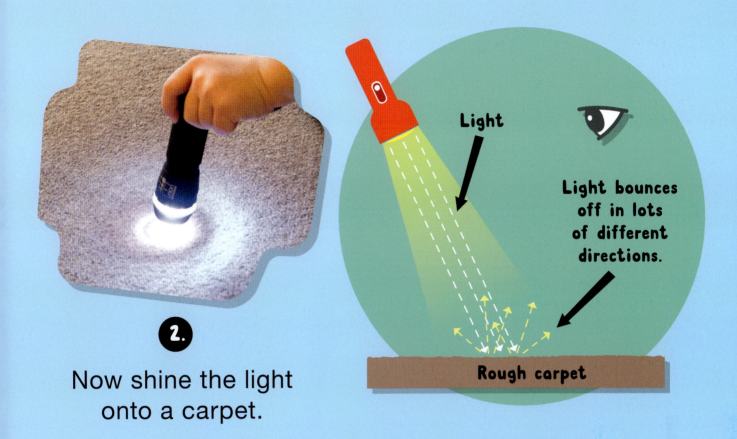

Light

Light bounces off in lots of different directions.

Rough carpet

2.

Now shine the light onto a carpet.

This is why smooth surfaces reflect light more cleanly than rough ones.

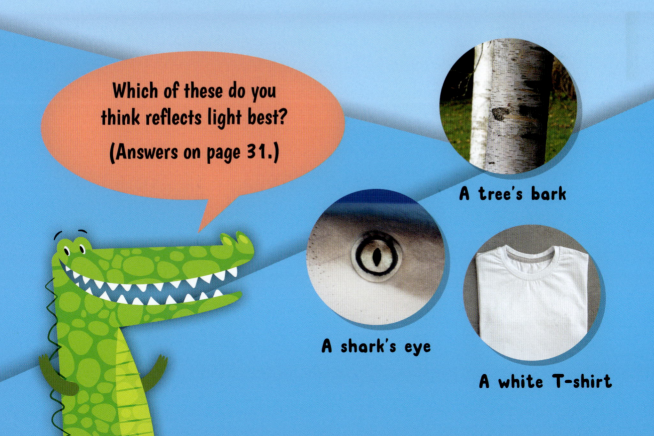

Which of these do you think reflects light best?

(Answers on page 31.)

A tree's bark

A shark's eye

A white T-shirt

MIRROR IMAGES

When I first saw a mirror, I thought there was another crocodile inside! But how do mirrors actually work?

When light hits the smooth surface inside a mirror, it bounces straight off. All the light bounces off in the same direction.

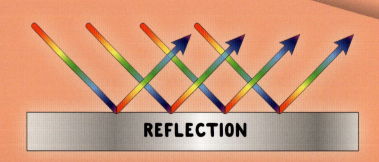

REFLECTION

Straight lines and angles

If the mirror is pointed straight at an object, that is what you see in the mirror. But if the mirror is at an **angle**, you see whatever is at that angle.

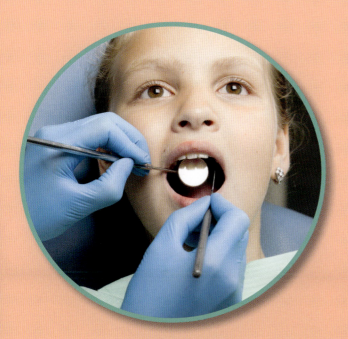

Now you know this, play around with a small mirror.

You could:

• Look at the person sitting next to you.

• Use the mirror to look behind you.

• Look at something on the ceiling or floor.

COLOURS

My favourite colour is red. Or maybe crocodile-green – that looks very smart! I wonder what makes something a particular colour?

Light is made up of different colours. When we look at a rainbow, we are seeing the colours that make up light.

Red

Orange

Yellow

Green

Blue

Indigo

Violet

When ALL the colours in light are together, they look white. But when light hits an object, all the colours don't always bounce off. Sometimes, only SOME colours bounce back to our eyes. The part of light that bounces back is what we see as colour.

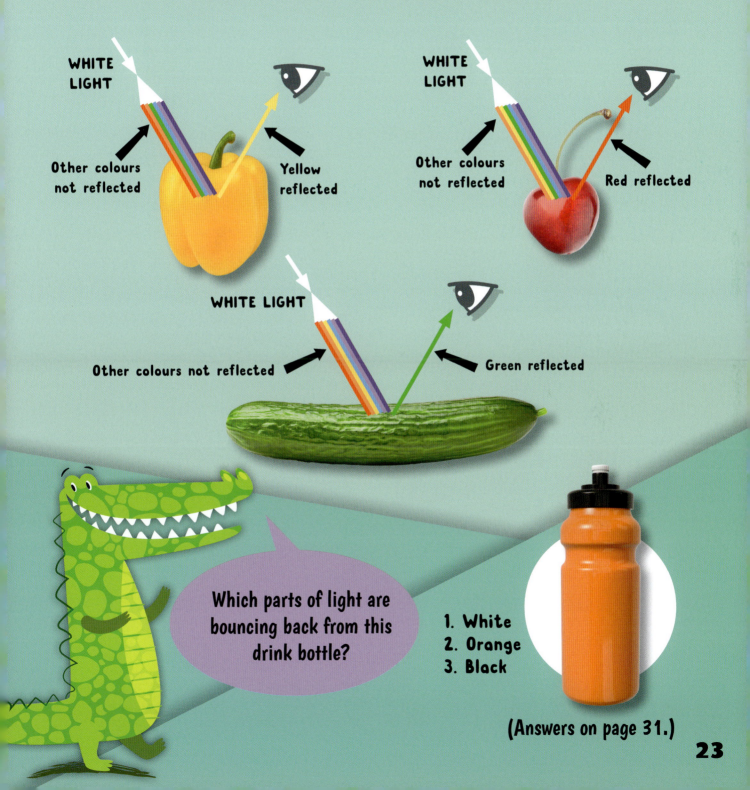

WHITE LIGHT

Other colours not reflected

Yellow reflected

WHITE LIGHT

Other colours not reflected

Red reflected

WHITE LIGHT

Other colours not reflected

Green reflected

Which parts of light are bouncing back from this drink bottle?

1. White
2. Orange
3. Black

(Answers on page 31.)

23

ANIMAL EYES

Crocodiles see differently from humans. Our eyes are built to be good at sticking out of the water, watching for **prey** along the riverbank.

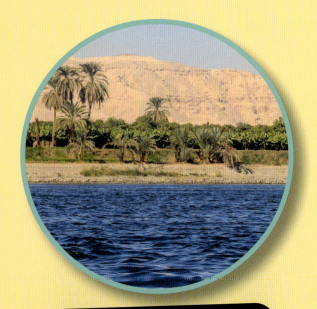

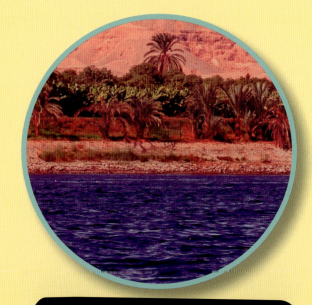

Human vision is good for seeing everything, but does not zoom in on anything particular.

Crocodile vision is very good for seeing prey on a riverbank. Freshwater crocodiles are specially good at seeing red.

Crocodiles are not the only animals that see light differently from humans. See if you can guess which animals these visions belong to. Find out if you guessed right on page 31.

Night colour

Humans find it hard to see when there is not much light around. Other animals specialise in seeing at night. Geckos, for example, can even see colours when it is almost dark:

Human vision in dark

Gecko vision in dark

Hello!

A

Human vision

?

B

Human vision

?

C

Human vision

?

1. Dog   2. Jumping spider   3. Giant clam

LIGHT AND LIFE

I couldn't live without light. Without sunlight's warmth, we crocodiles (and other reptiles) get too cold and die. Crocodiles are not alone: few living things could survive without light.

Plants

Plants use light (plus water and a **gas** called carbon dioxide) to make their own food. Without light, plants would have no food.

Animals

If there was no light, animals that eat plants would soon have nothing to eat. Soon after that, animals that eat other animals would have nothing to eat either.

Some animals do live without light:

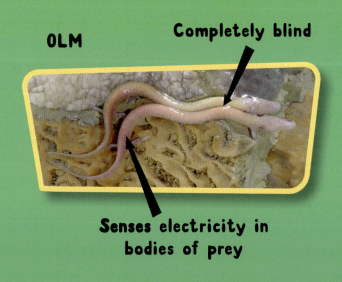

OLM

Completely blind

Senses electricity in bodies of prey

Humans

Humans need sunlight to stay healthy. Sunshine makes our bodies produce vitamin D.

+ **=** VITAMIN D

Vitamin D keeps your bones, muscles and teeth healthy.

DUMBO OCTOPUS

BLIND MEXICAN TETRA FISH

Fins look (a bit) like Dumbo's ears. Lives in deep ocean where no light reaches.

Lives in dark caves in Mexico. Eyes have completely disappeared.

WORK IT OUT

Based on what you've learned about light, heat and colour, see if you can work out the answers to these questions. For a change, the answers are upside-down below the photos.

If you wanted to see around a corner, how could you do this?

Why do people in hot countries often wear white clothes?

A little mirror would be a good tool. You can buy little mirrors on telescopic poles, which would be perfect.

When something looks white, you know that it is reflecting every colour of light. So white clothes reflect as much light and heat as possible.

Why are solar panels black?

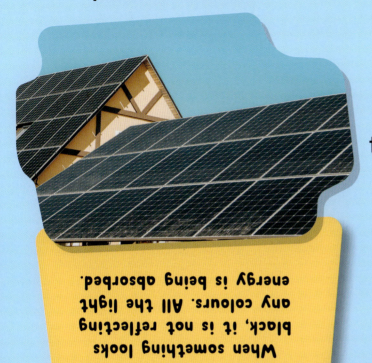

When something looks black, it is not reflecting any colours. All the light energy is being absorbed.

Why do ripe tomatoes look red?

And what would a ripe tomato look like if you looked at it through a green **filter** (which lets through only green light)?

Ripe tomatoes look red because they reflect red light back to our eyes.

If we looked at them through a green filter, no red light would get through — so the tomatoes would look black.

What might happen to your bones if you stayed indoors all the time?

They would get weaker and more likely to break, because without sunlight your body would stop producing vitamin D, which makes our bones strong.

 # GLOSSARY

angle size of a corner between one line and another. Lines that make a big corner have a 'wide' angle. Lines that make a pointy corner have a 'narrow' angle

atoms the tiny building blocks of which everything is made

energy ability to do something physical

filter thin skin or film that lets some things (for example, red light) through but not others

freshwater water in streams, rivers and lakes, which does not have a salty taste

gas something that spreads out and fills whatever space it is in. Air is made up of gases

latch fastening for a door

light sources objects that light comes from

muscle part of the body that is used to move arms, legs and other parts

prey animal that is hunted and killed by other animals for food

reflection bouncing back of light (or heat, or sound) from the surface of an object

sense be aware of an event or object

shade area of shadow behind an object, where less (or no) light reaches

telescopic with parts that fit inside each other, which can be pulled out to make it longer

tilt lean or topple to the side

tomb underground space where the body of someone who has died is put

vision being able to see

ANSWERS

Pages 6–7

1 No light is reaching the page, so you cannot read anything. **2** You can see words, and perhaps read them, because the hole is letting in light. **3** You can see light in the tube but probably not much else, because the light is coming from further away and less is reaching the page.

Pages 8–9

1 Yes, lightbulbs are a light source. **2** Firefly: yes. **3** Cat's eyes: no, these bounce light back. **4** Bicycle light: yes. Reflector: no. **5** Angler fish: yes. **6** Phone screen: yes. **7** Solar tower: no.

Page 19

Shark's eyes have a special, light-reflecting layer inside, so this would be best. Tree bark is very rough, so the light would bounce off it in lots of directions and this would probably be worst. A white T-shirt looks smooth from far away, but up close is not, so this would probably be in the middle.

Page 23

1 white is all the colours bouncing back, **2** orange is a combination of red and yellow, **3** black is NONE of the colours bouncing back.

Pages 24–25

2A: jumping spiders have excellent vision and can even see kinds of light that humans cannot.

3B: this is what the world looks like to a giant clam, looking through the hundreds of tiny eyes along its side.

1C: this is how a dog sees the world. Dogs can see well, but do not see red.

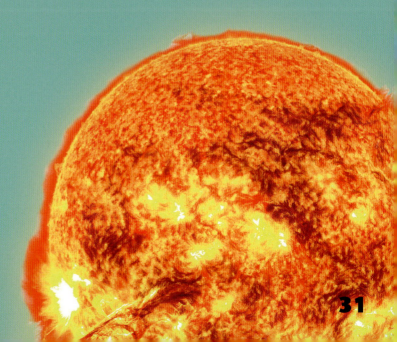

FINDING OUT MORE

Books to read

***Science in a Flash: Light* Georgina Amson-Bradshaw (Franklin Watts, 2018).** Every time you turn a new page, you meet one of ten 'flash' facts about light. Read on, and you find out more about that particular fact.

***Spectacular Light and Sound* Rob Colson and Jon Richards (Wayland, 2019).** Attention-grabbing facts and explanations about extreme forms of light and sound, from the loudest bangs to the kind of light that lets you look inside a human body.

***Why Does a Mirror Show Things Back to Front? And Other Questions About Light* Anna Claybourne (Wayland, 2020).** The questions this book asks will get your attention – and the answers it gives will fill your brain with loads of impressive facts about light.

Websites to visit

bbc.co.uk/bitesize/primary
If you dig into the site, there's a lot of content here, often explained using videos and interactive games. You can just use the search function to look for 'light'.

ducksters.com
Click on 'Science', then 'Physics', then look under the Light and optics, then Intro to light to find basic information about light. You can also find out about telescopes, how lenses (for example, in eyeglasses) work and more. This website is quite serious, but it's a good place to find out information quickly.

INDEX

A
animals 26, 27
atoms 4, 5, 10

C
colours 22, 23, 28, 29

D
darkness 11, 16, 18

E
Earth 10, 11, 12, 13
energy 4

H
heat 5, 9, 11, 12, 13, 16, 28

L
light sources 8, 9, 14, 15, 16

M
mirrors 20, 21, 28

N
night 10, 11

P
plants 26

R
rainbow 22
reflections 18, 19, 21, 28

S
seasons 12, 13
seeing 4, 6, 24, 25
shadows 16, 17
Sun 5, 8, 10, 11, 12, 13, 14, 16

V
vision 24, 25
vitamin D 27, 29